When I started felting, I had no idea I would travel such an interesting journey. My first scarf was a revelation to me. I couldn't believe the wool fibers were so reactive to water and soap and the end result was not only warm and durable, but stunning!

It was the start of my love affair with wool; one that has led me down many pleasurable paths of discovery.

I have experimented with colours and have learned about the different types of wool fibers from teachers and fellow felters. It's a wonderful community and I love to chat in the studio to people and share my knowledge. Please enjoy this book of my work and drop me a line if you'd like to talk about techniques, or share your story.

Warmest woolly regards,

Marta Madison

Marta Madison
Sydney, 2015

I0829223

www.silksation.wordpress.com
www.martamadison.wix.com/fashionillustrator
Silksation Silk Scarves
PO Box 491 Crows Nest NSW 1585 AUSTRALIA
mmadison@gmx.com +612 419 251 705
facebook.com/silksationscarves

All projects in this book are made with 100% merino wool and yarn sourced from NSW sheep farms, then decorated with fabric embellishments or nuno-felted onto hand-dyed silk.

Photography: Artur Ferrao www.arturferraophotographer.com

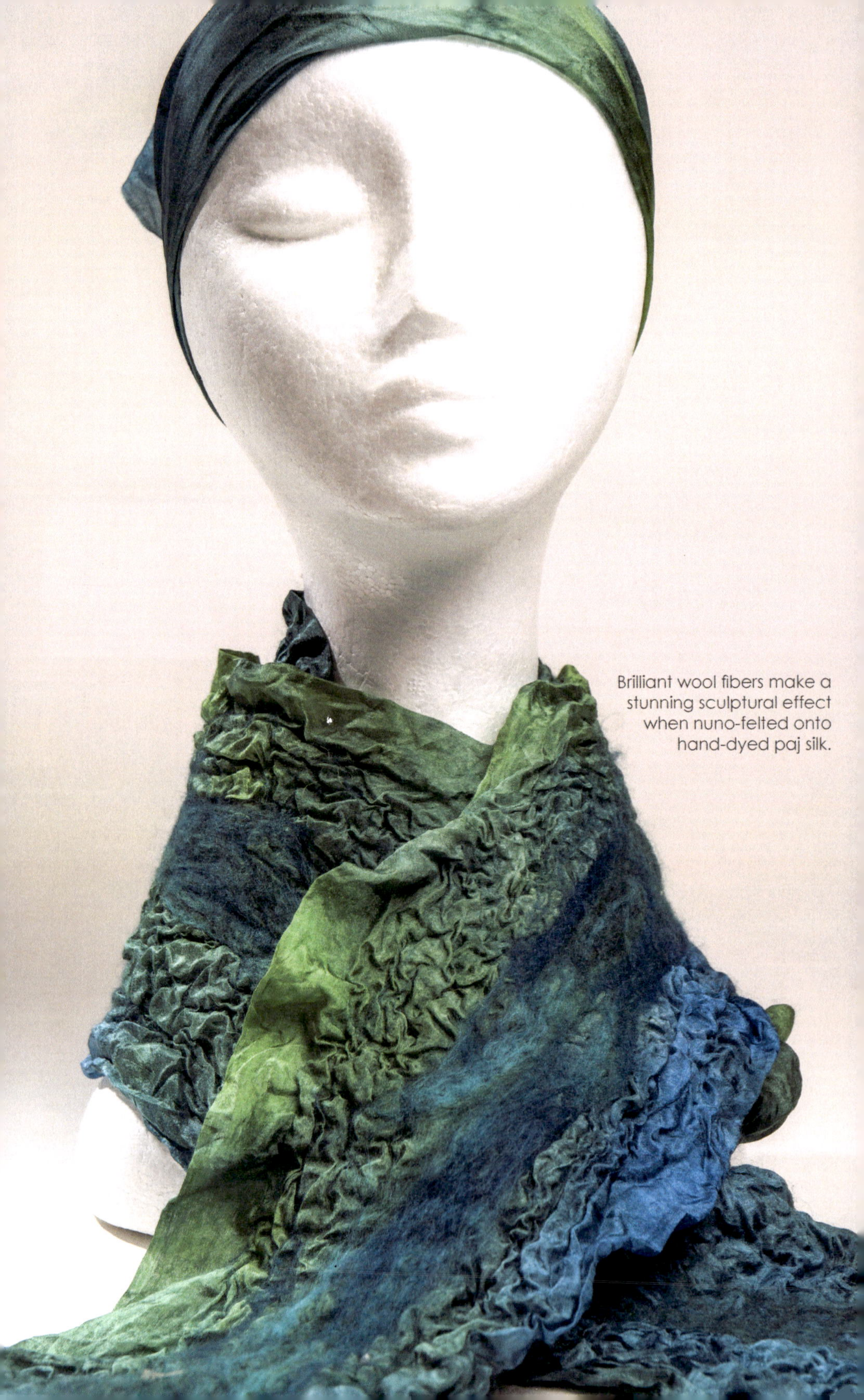

Brilliant wool fibers make a stunning sculptural effect when nuno-felted onto hand-dyed paj silk.

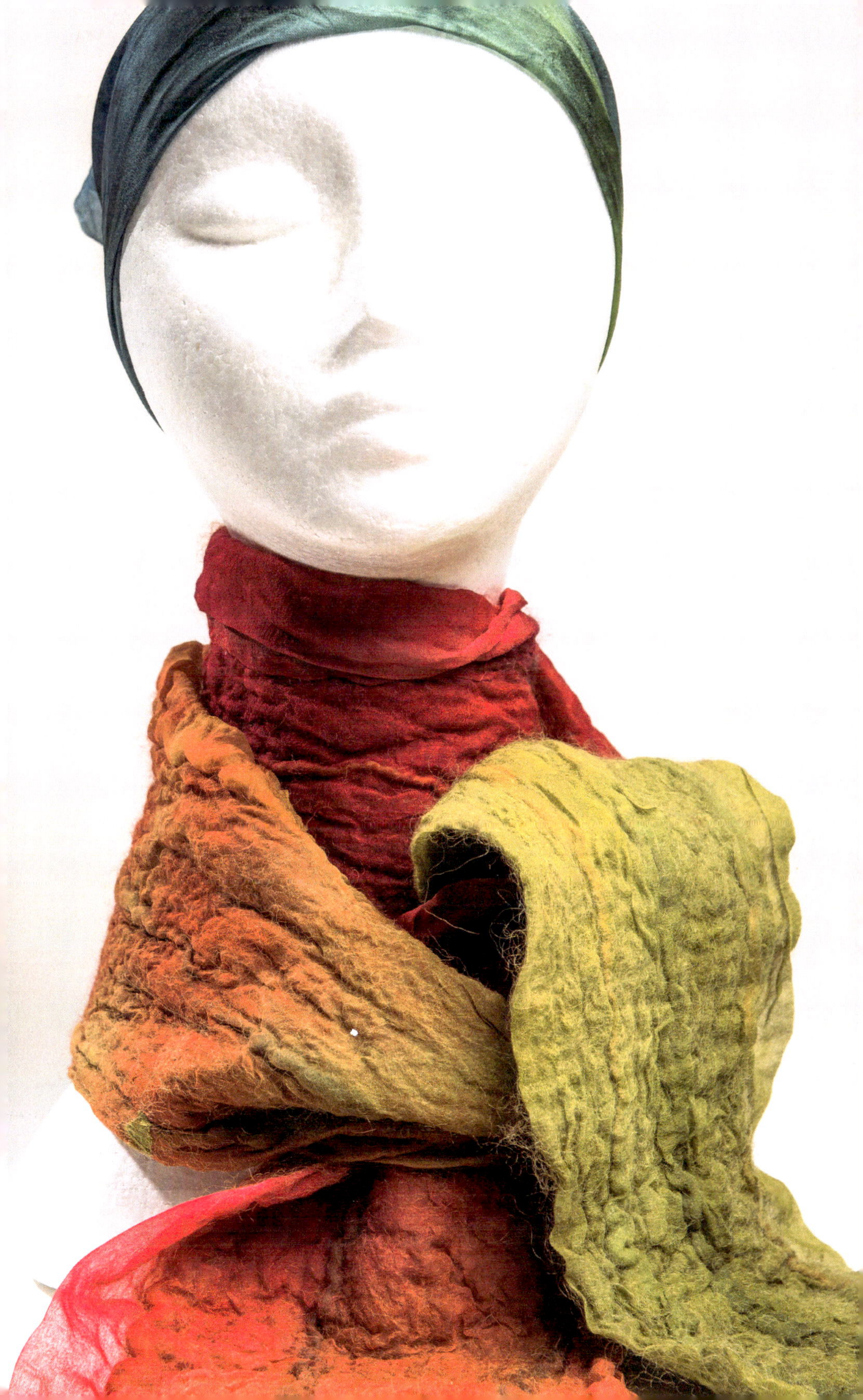

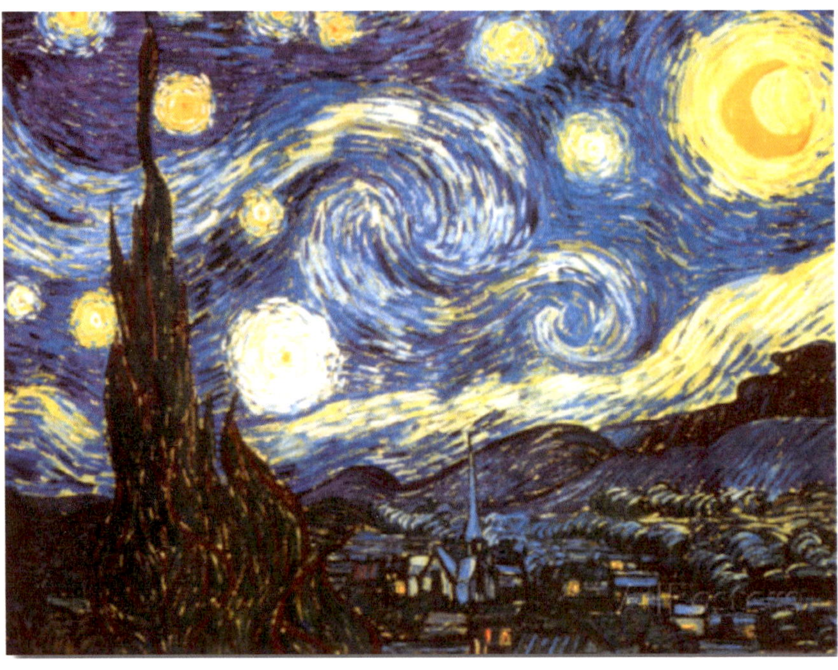

Scarf, inspired by Van Gogh's Starry Night painting (above). Yarn strands, 100% wool.

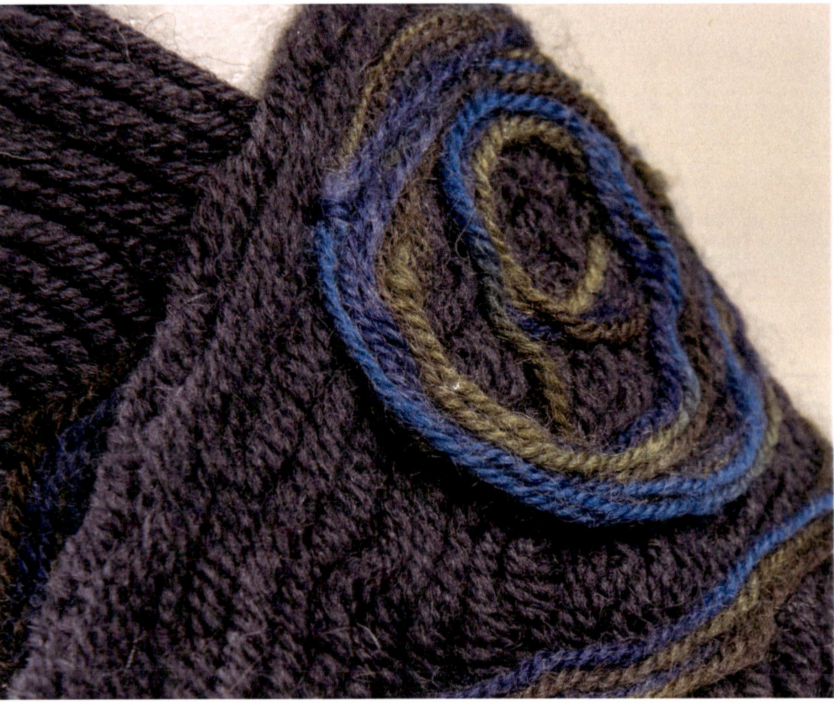

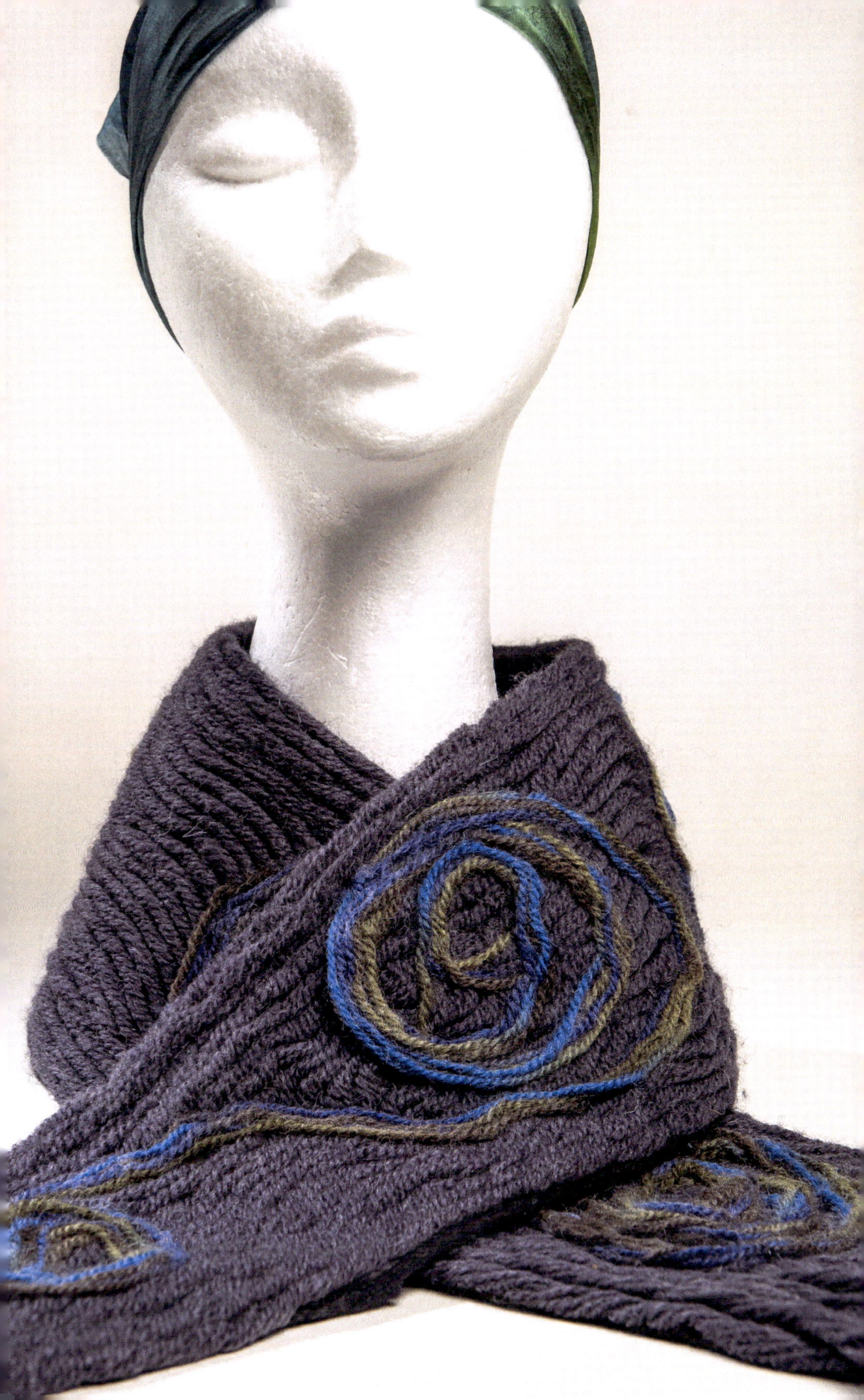

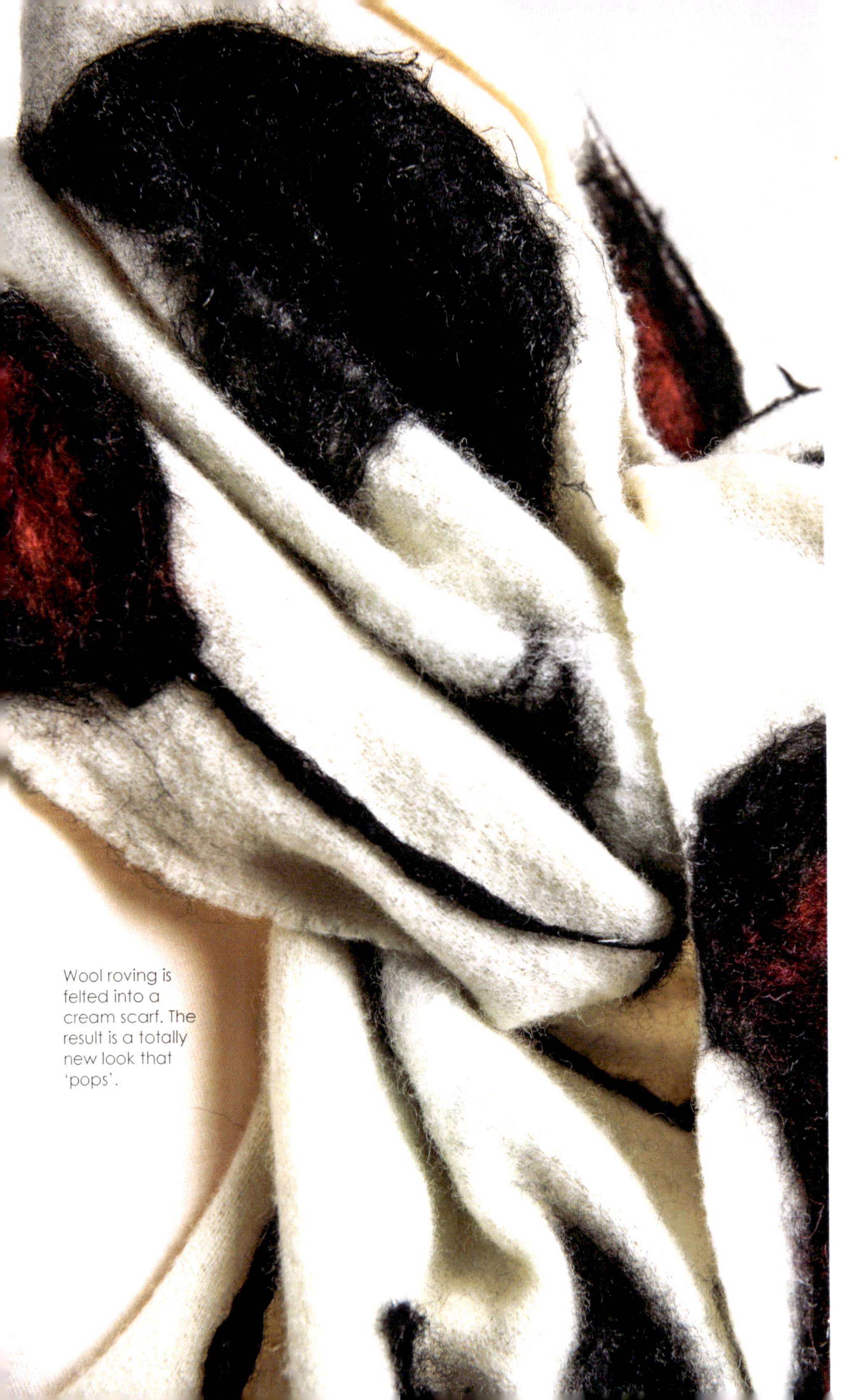

Wool roving is felted into a cream scarf. The result is a totally new look that 'pops'.

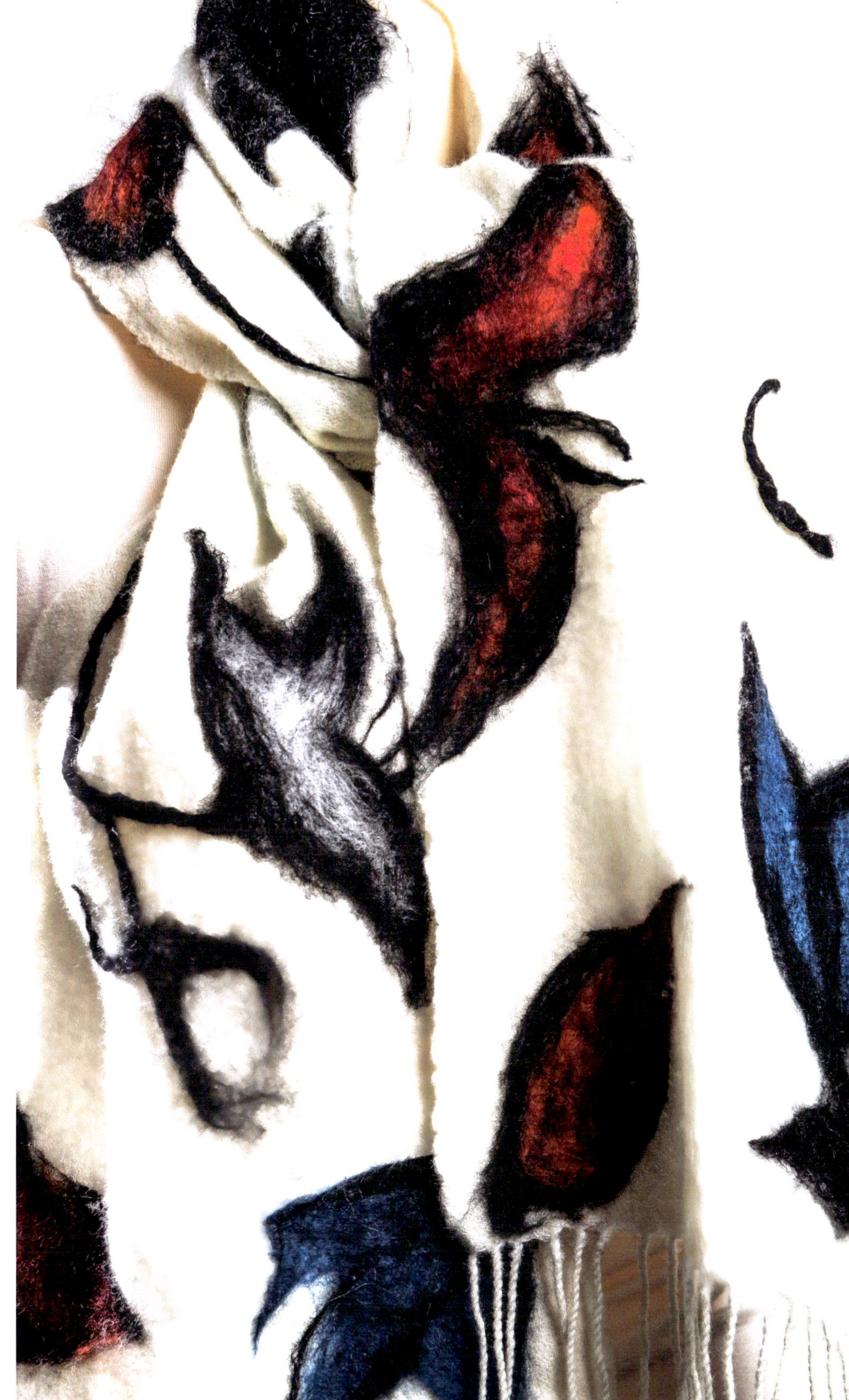

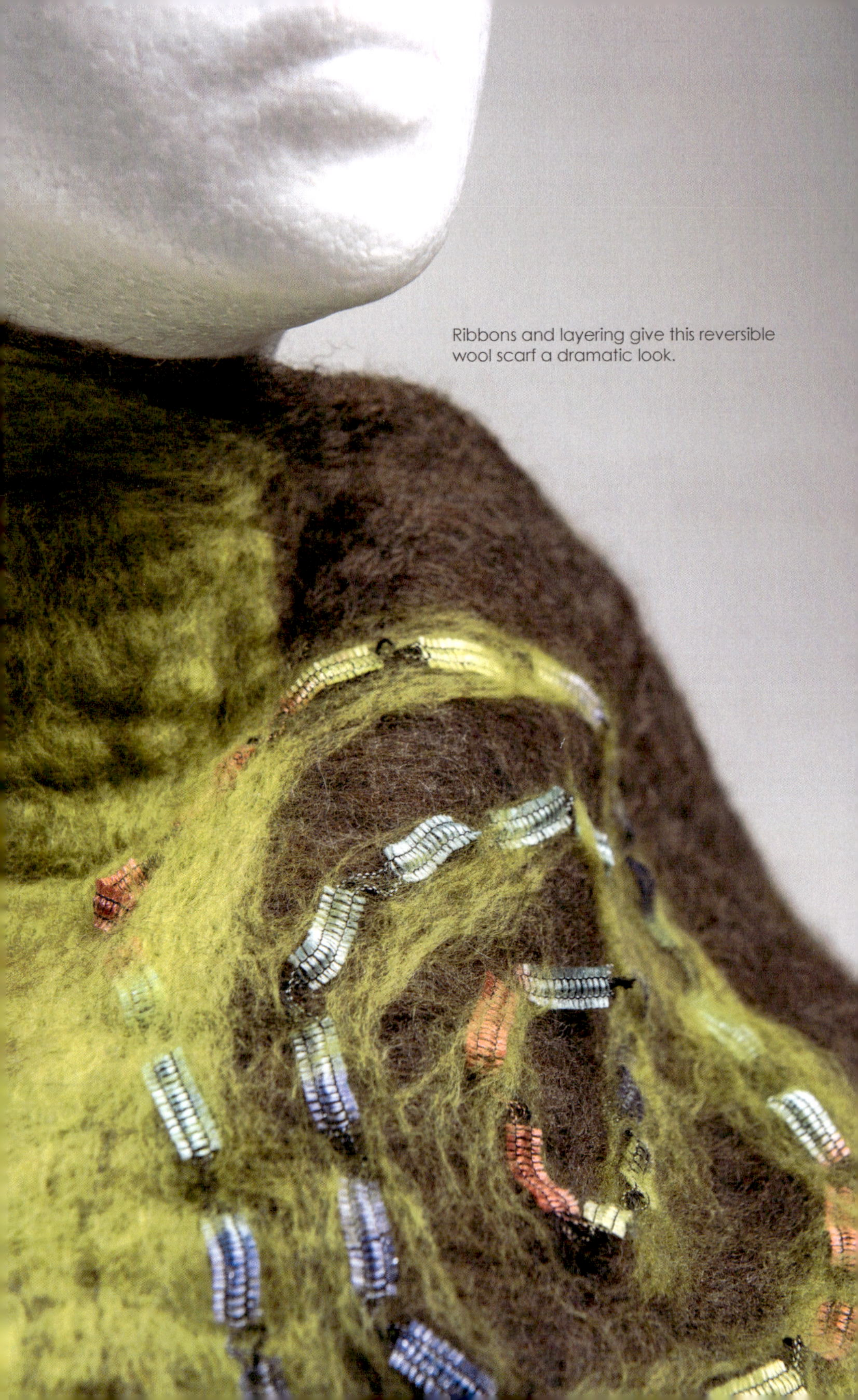

Ribbons and layering give this reversible wool scarf a dramatic look.

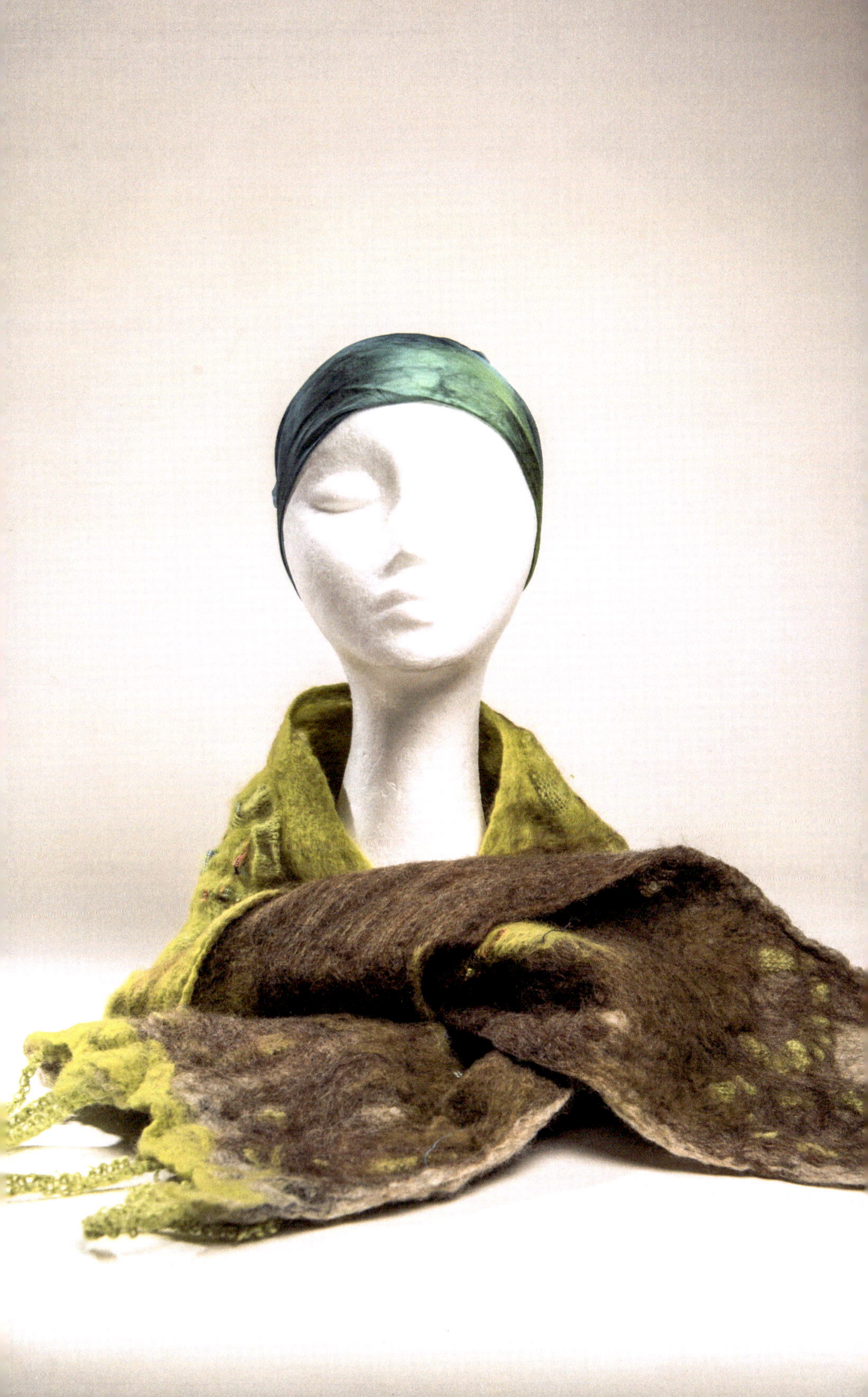

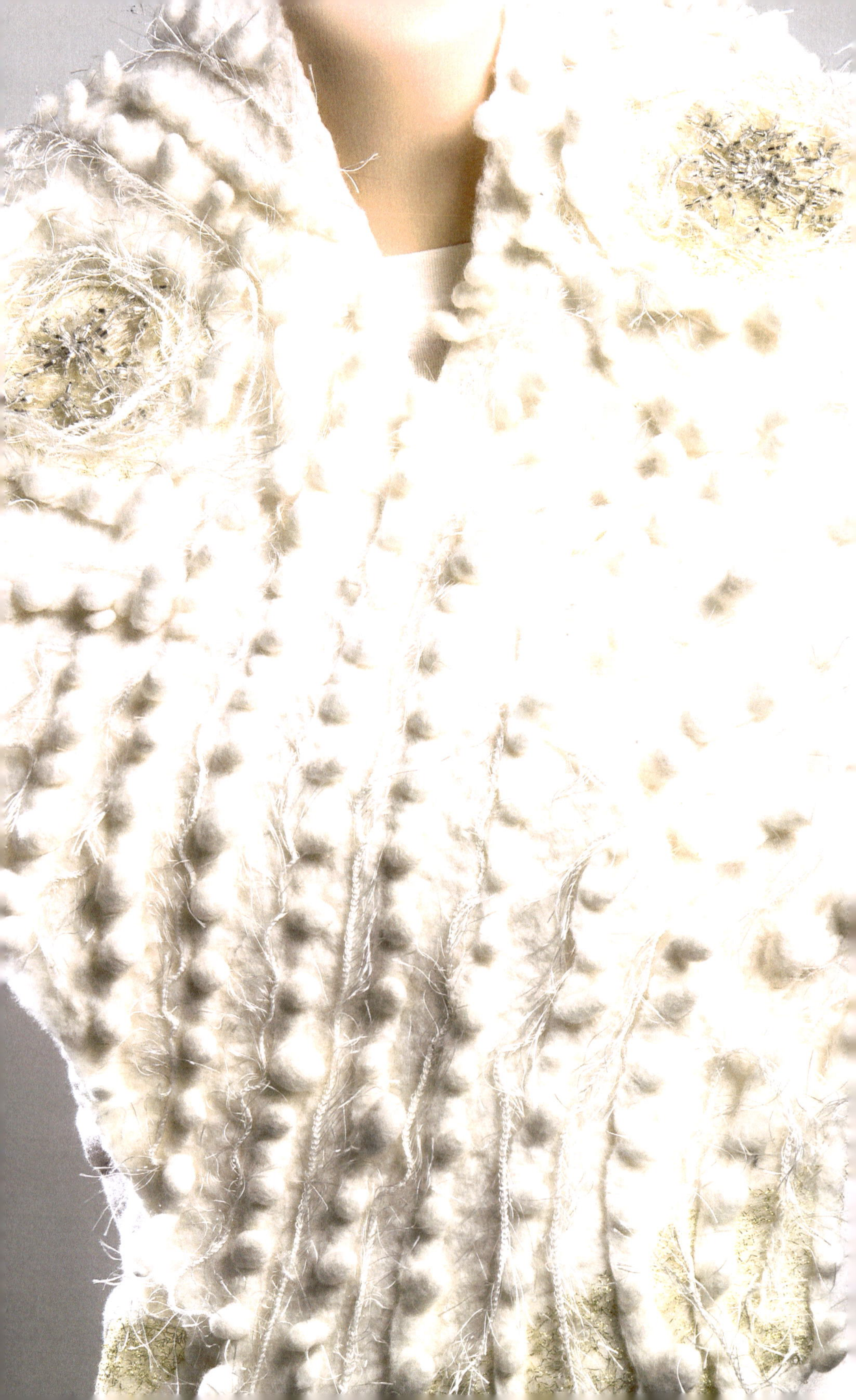

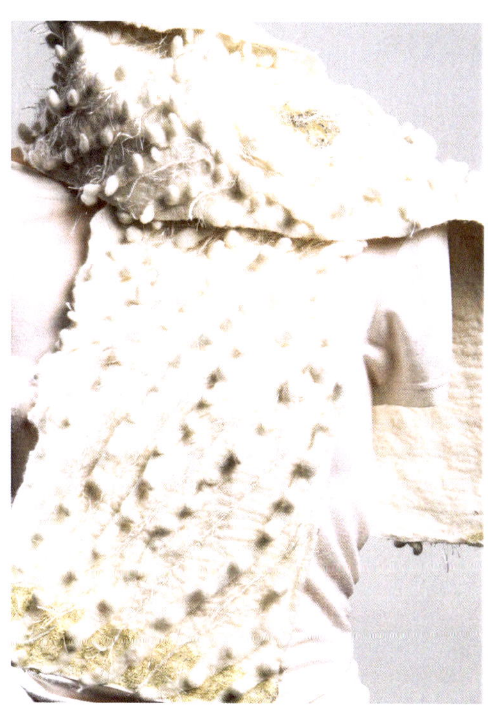

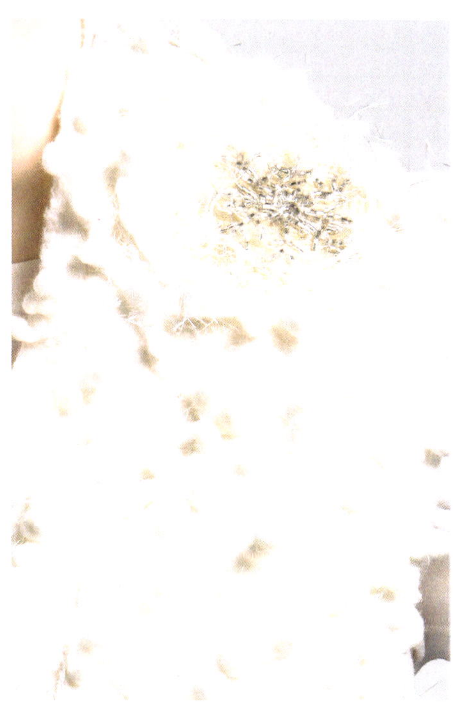

Wedding scarf #1:
In my series of wedding scarves, a special technique pushes the wool into loops; then gold and silver fibers are felted into the wool, giving it a truly ceremonial feel.

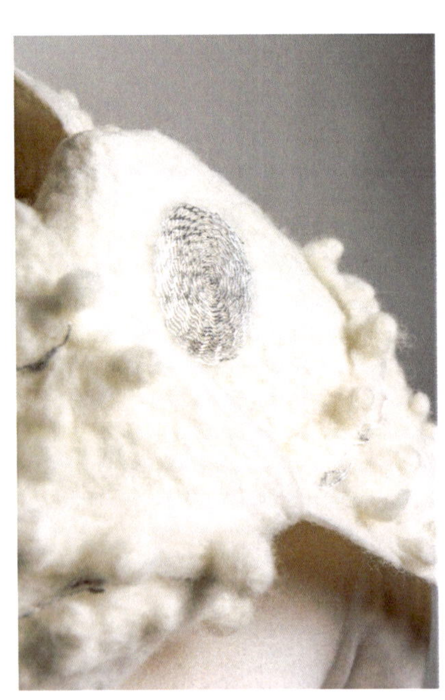

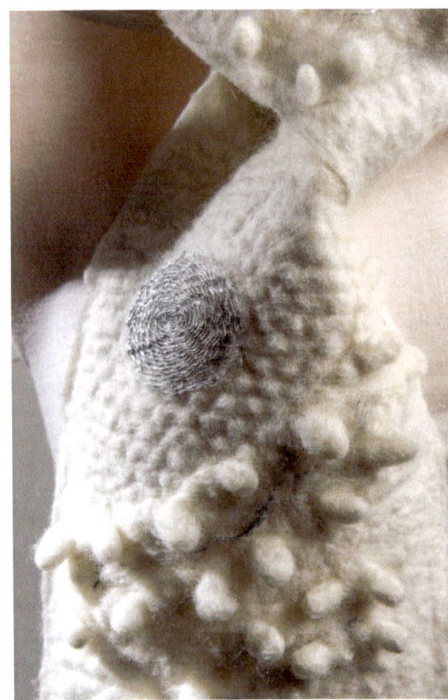

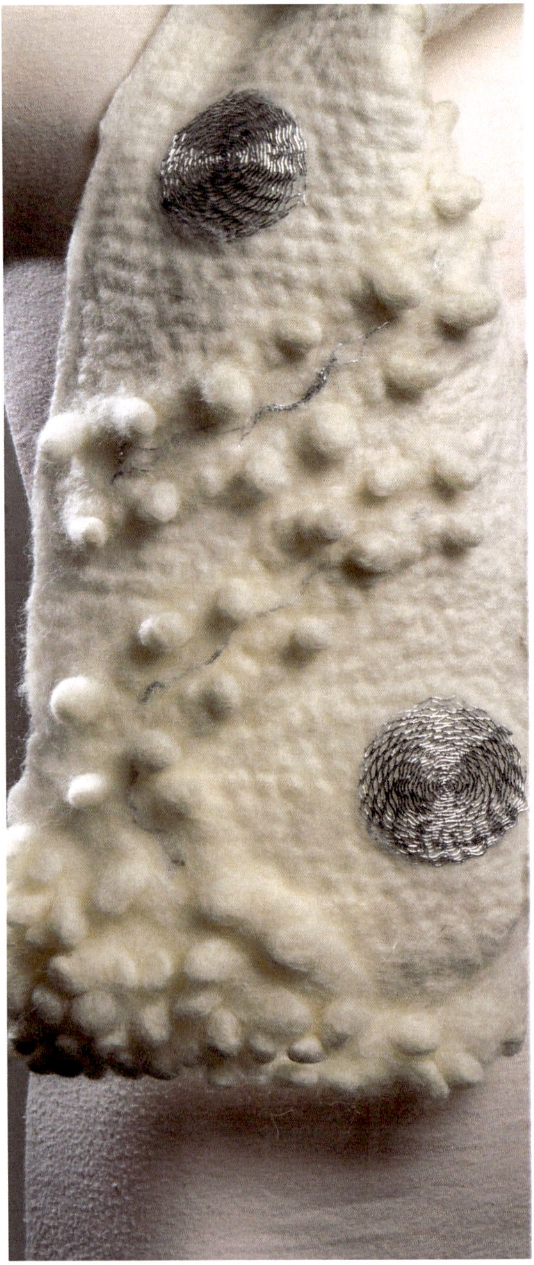

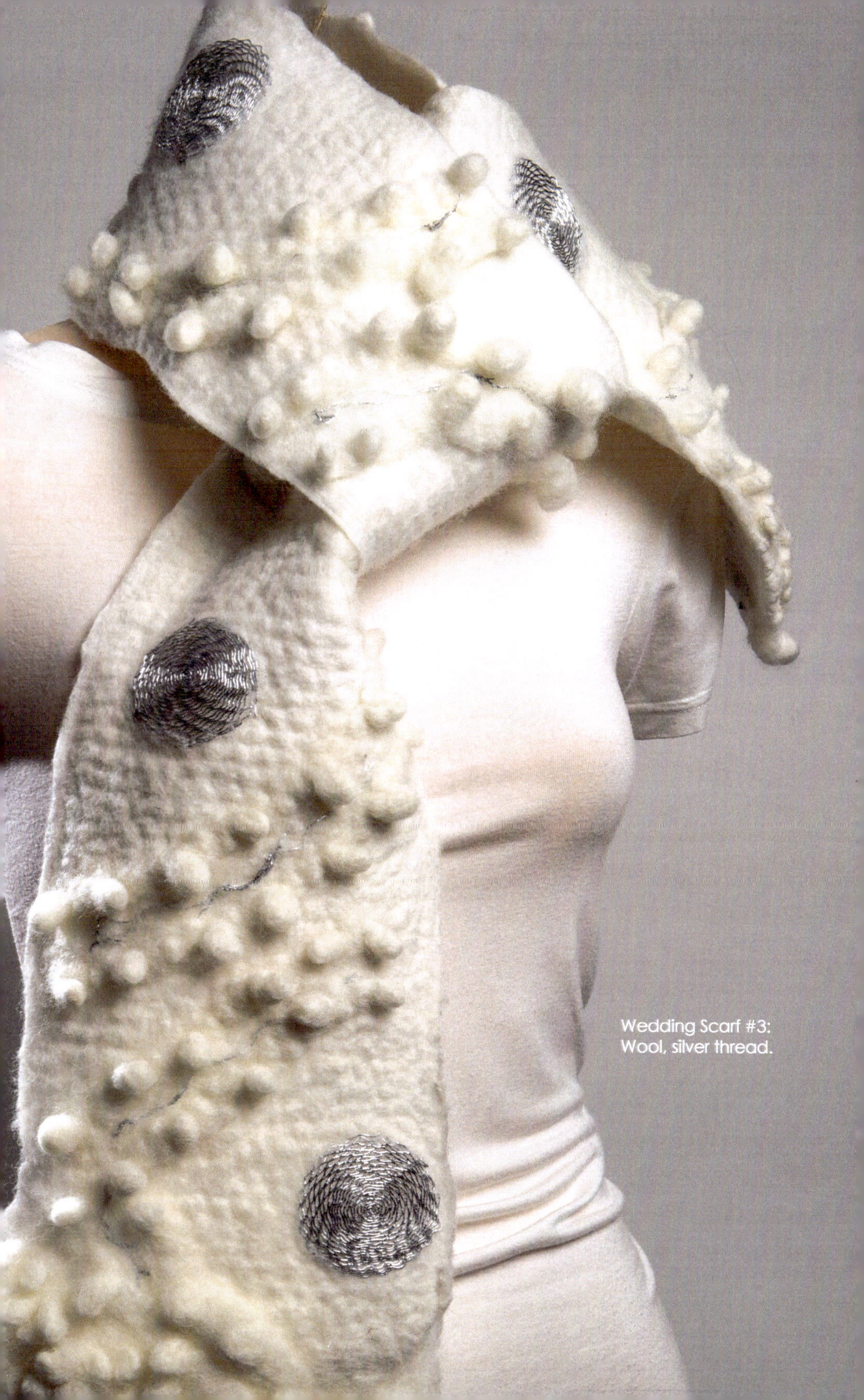

Wedding Scarf #3:
Wool, silver thread.

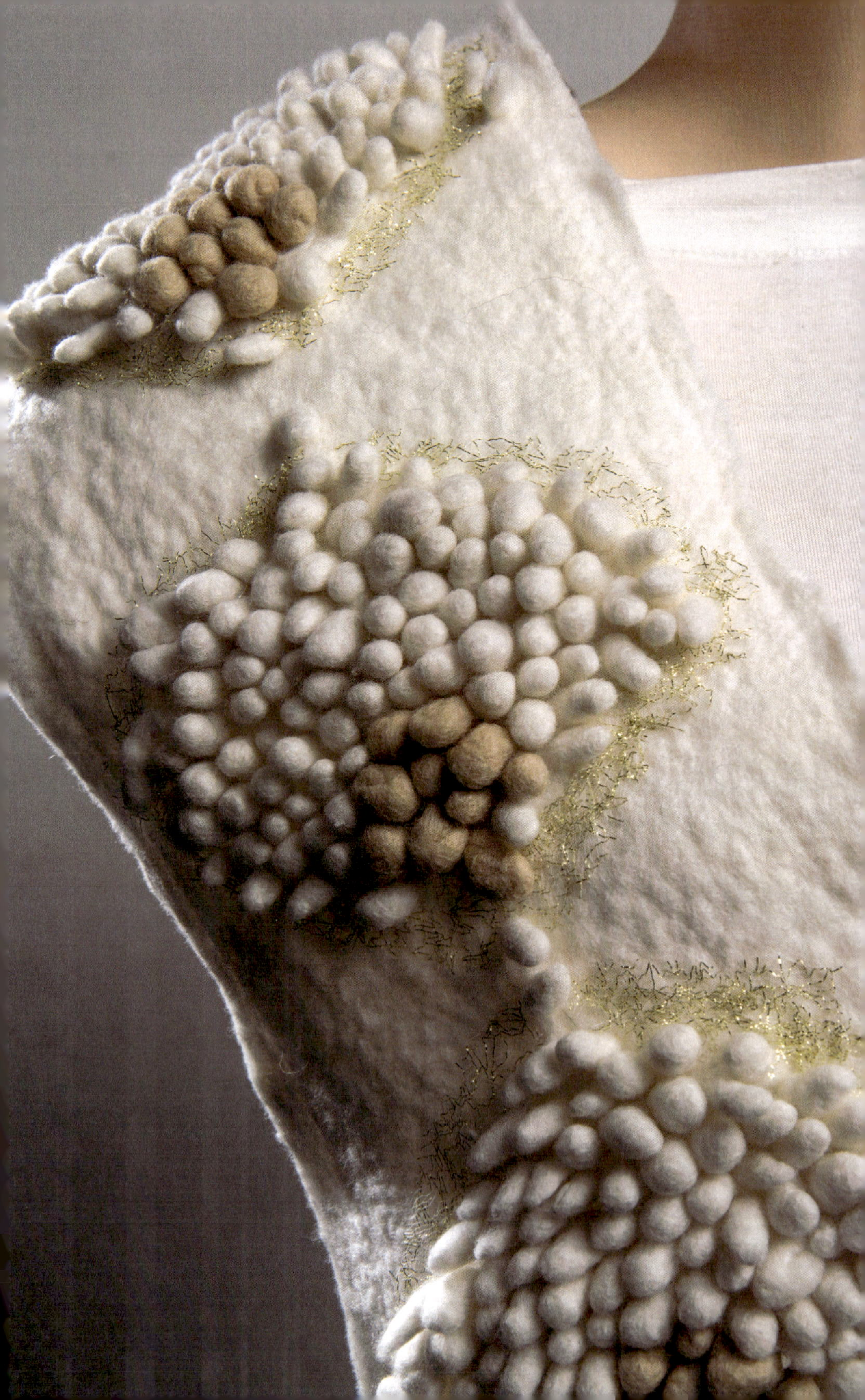

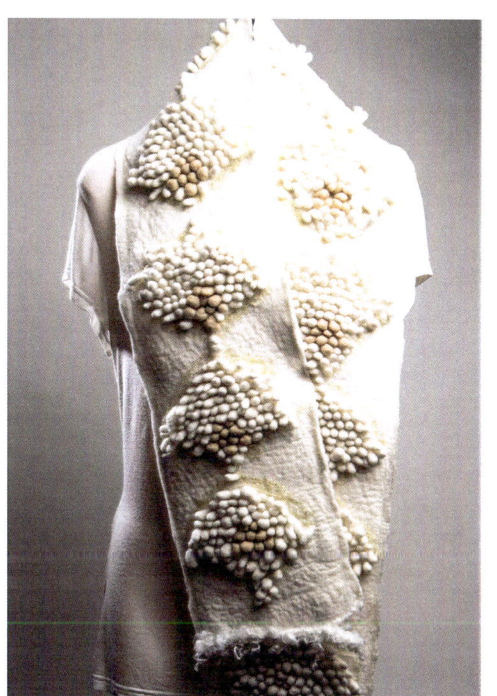

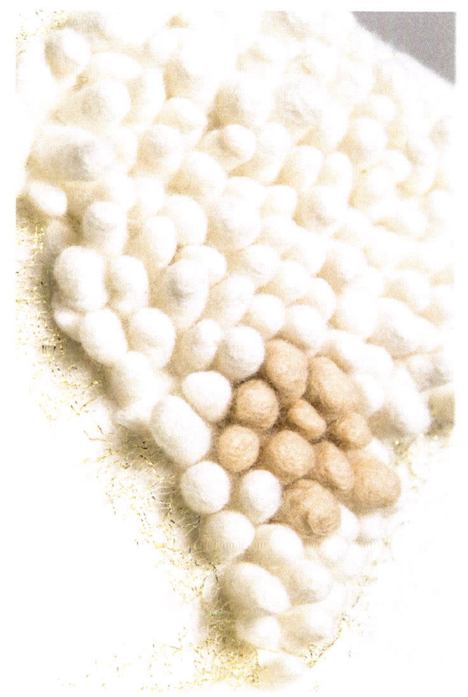

Wedding scarf #3:
There are many variations in the looping technique, which make for stunning textural effects.

Red and black

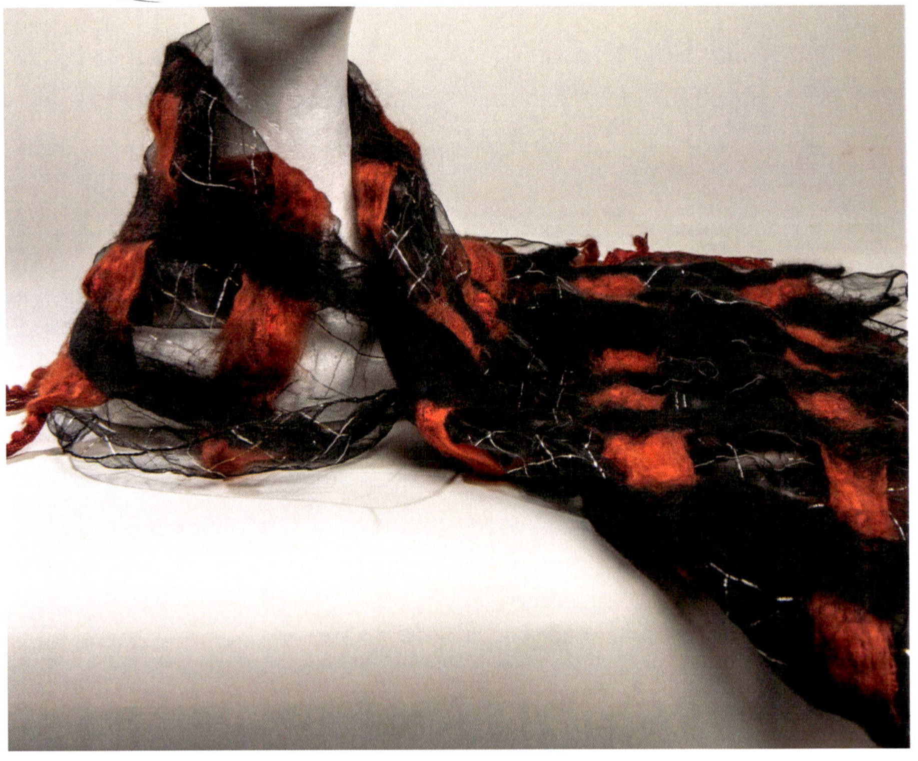

Wool, nuno-felted onto silk georgette, with silver thread.

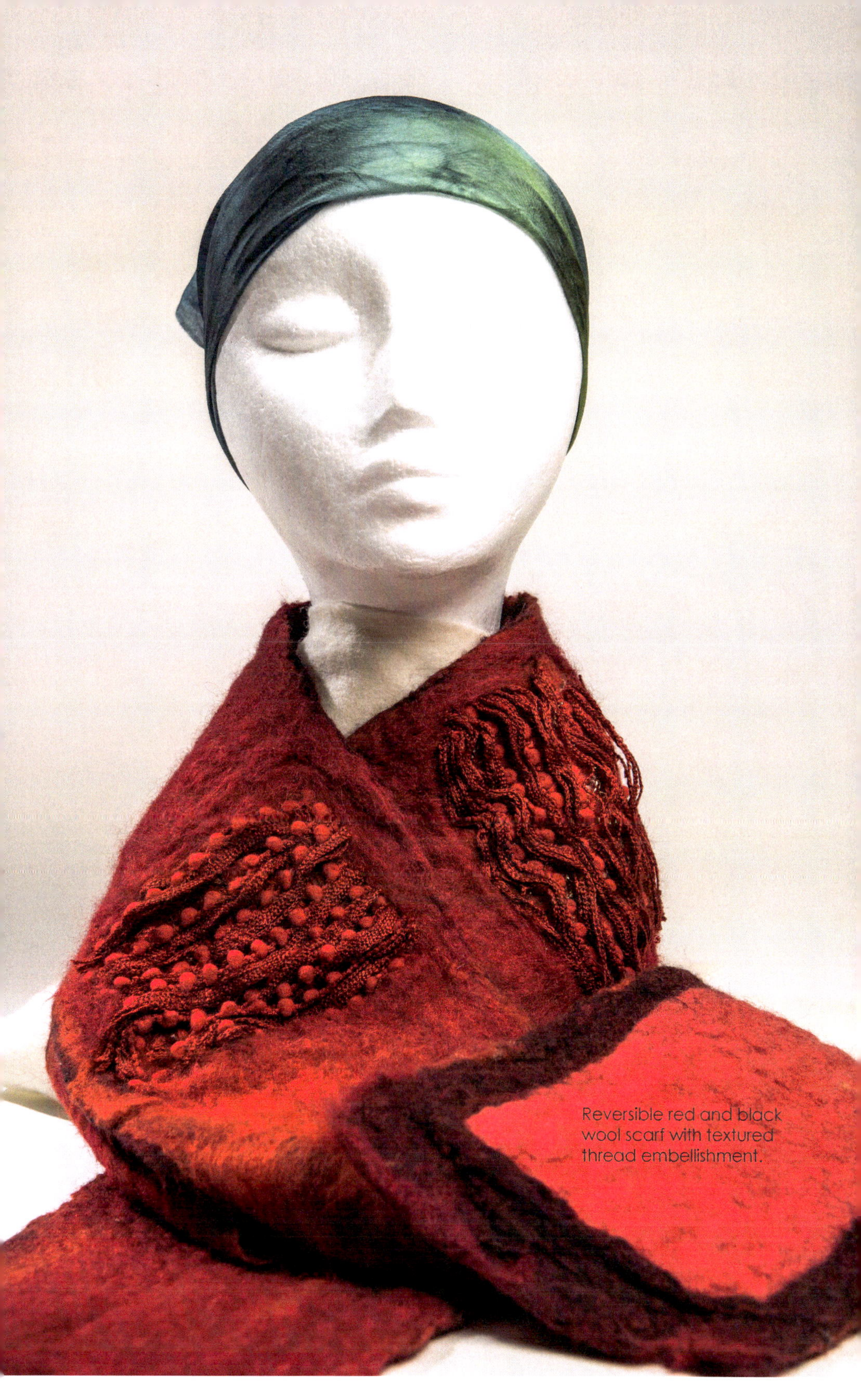

Reversible red and black wool scarf with textured thread embellishment.

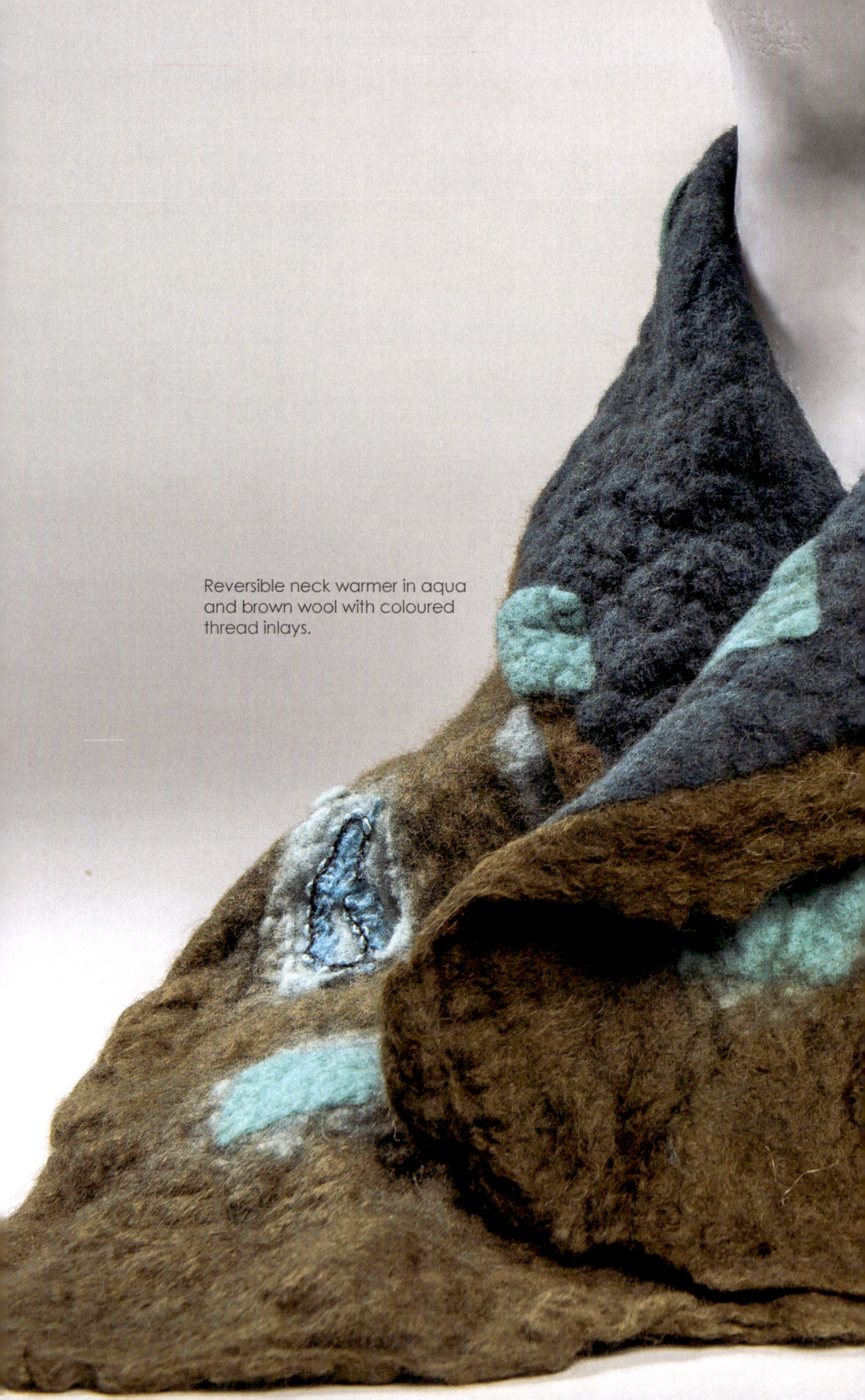

Reversible neck warmer in aqua and brown wool with coloured thread inlays.

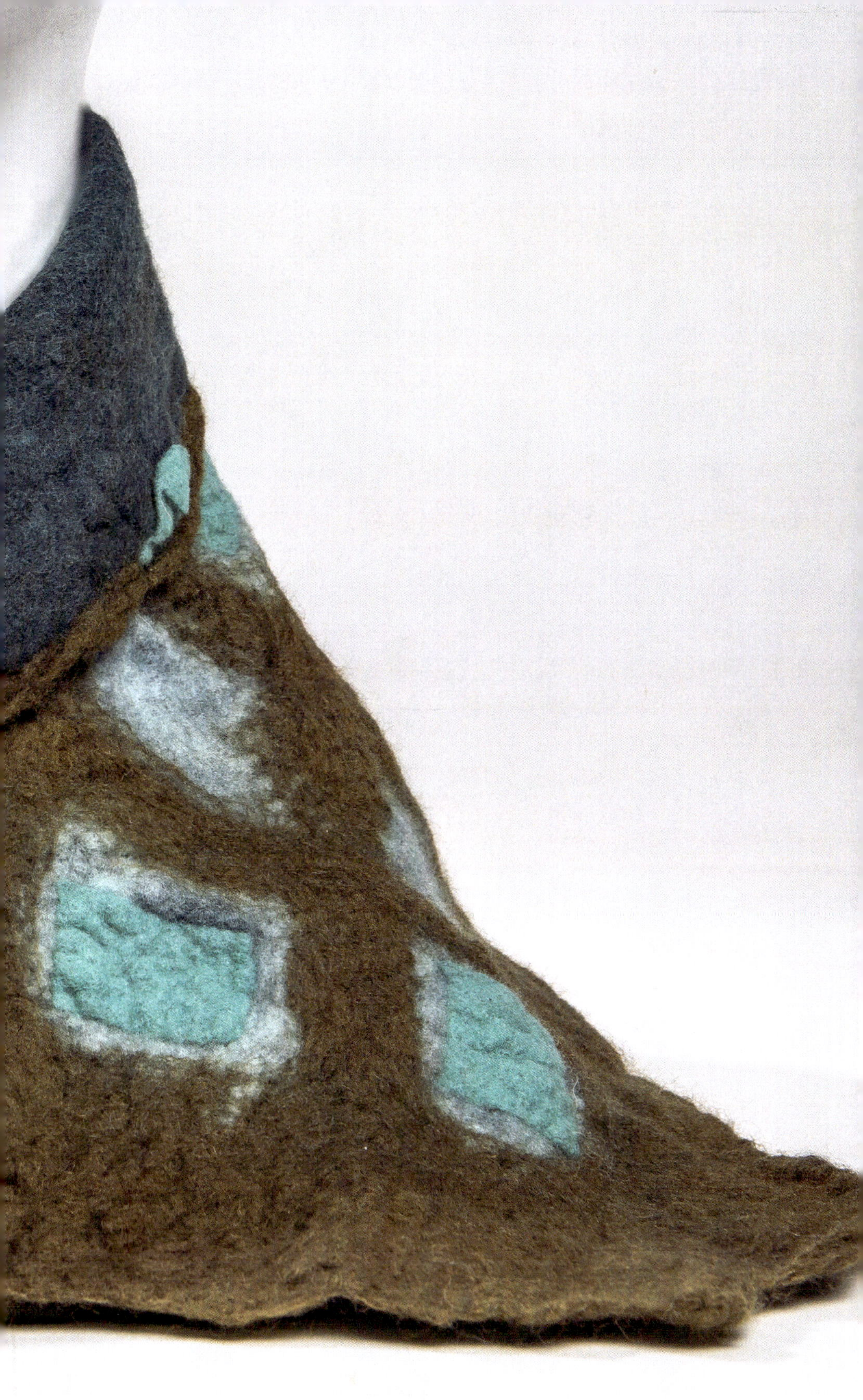

Shades of blue

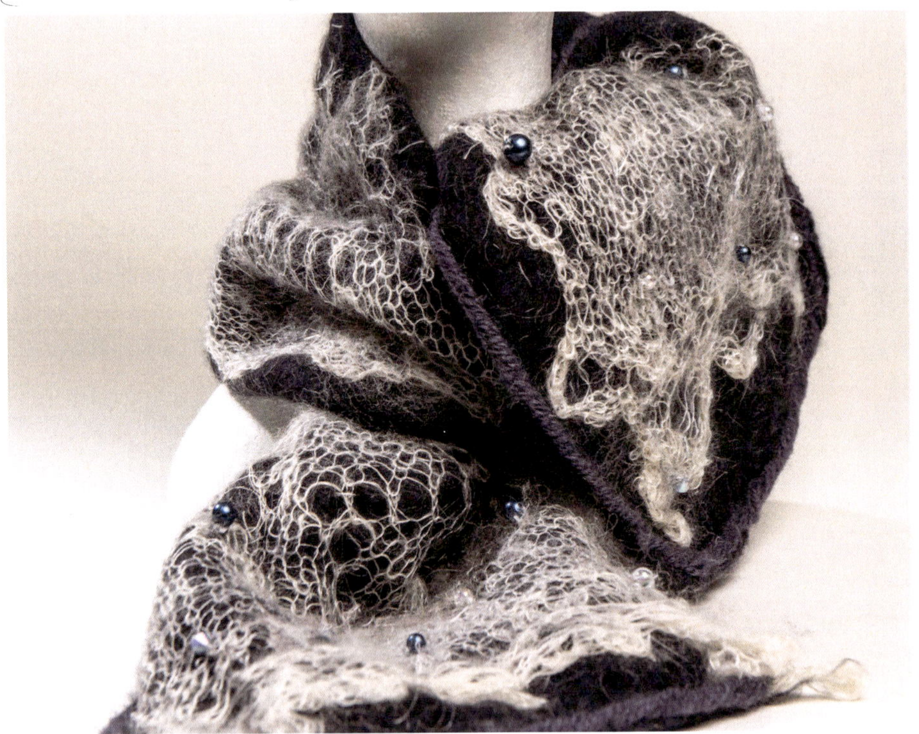

Crochet cream lace felted onto deep blue wool, decorated with pearl buttons.

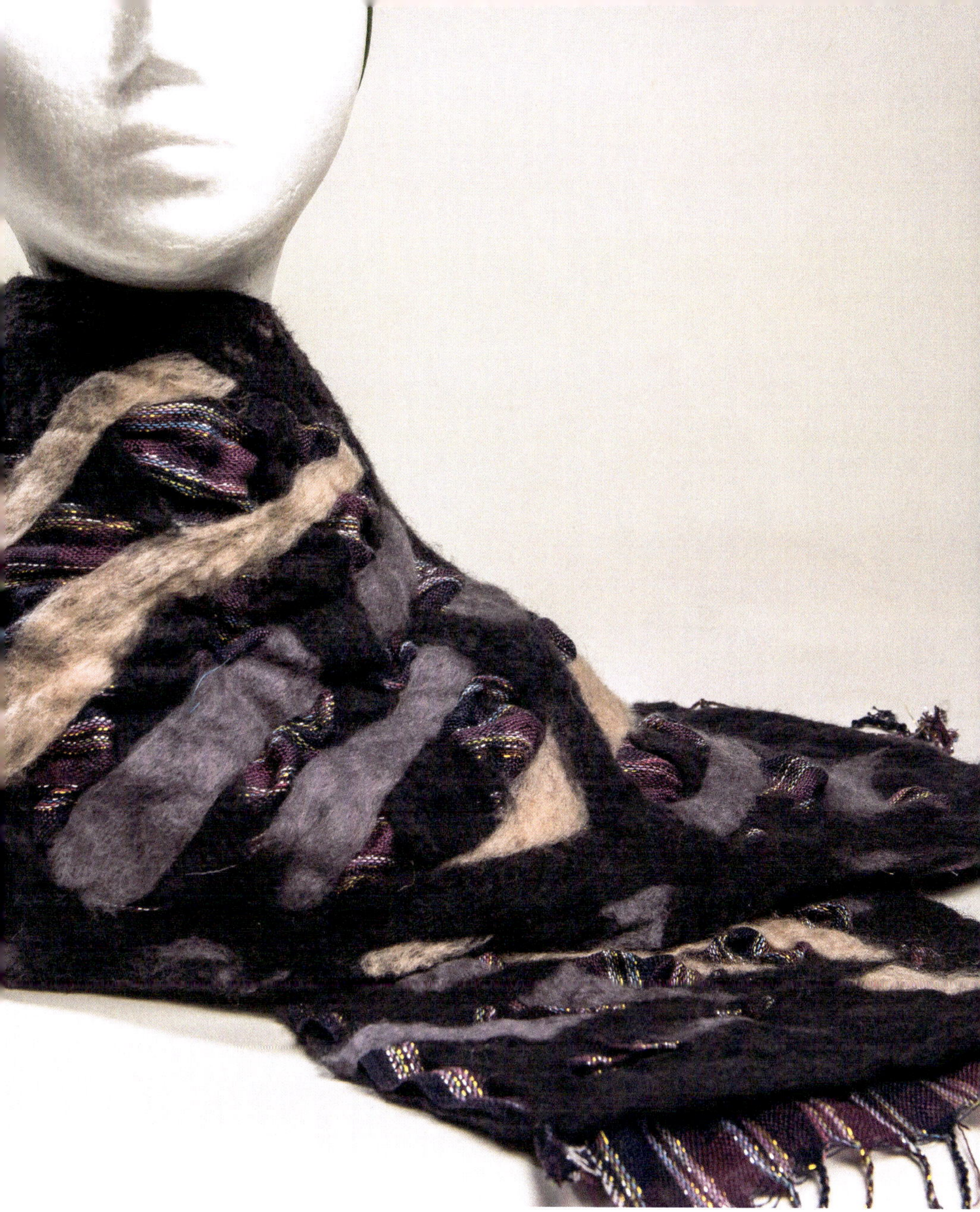

Triple layer blue wool, cotton stripe fabric, plaited roving and fringe.

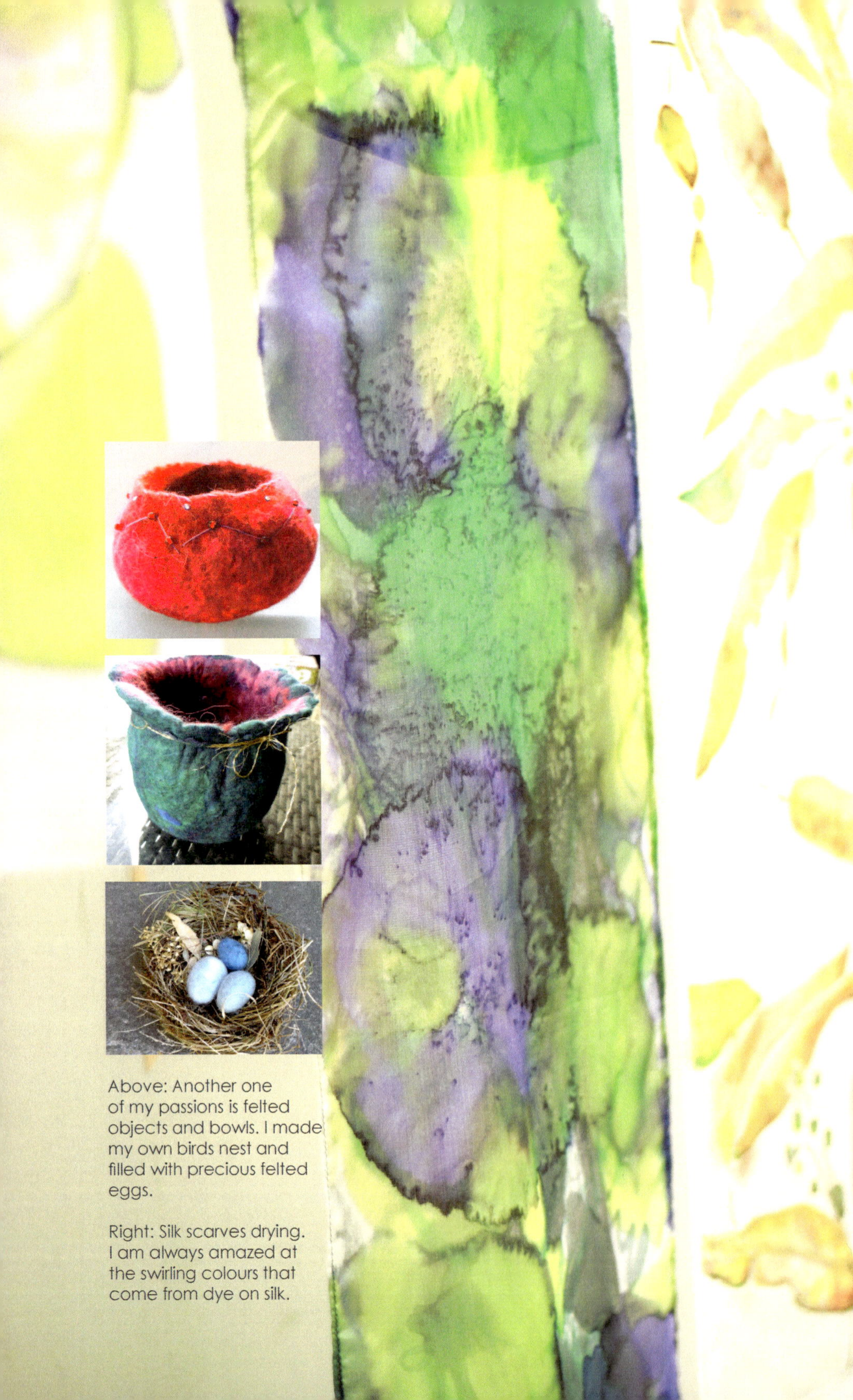

Above: Another one of my passions is felted objects and bowls. I made my own birds nest and filled with precious felted eggs.

Right: Silk scarves drying. I am always amazed at the swirling colours that come from dye on silk.

In the studio

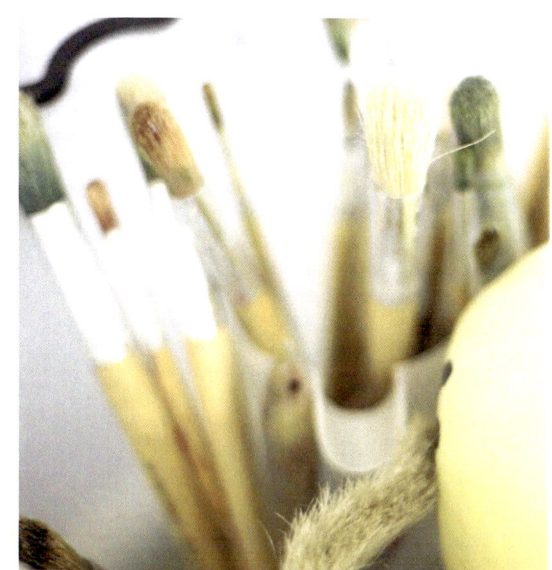

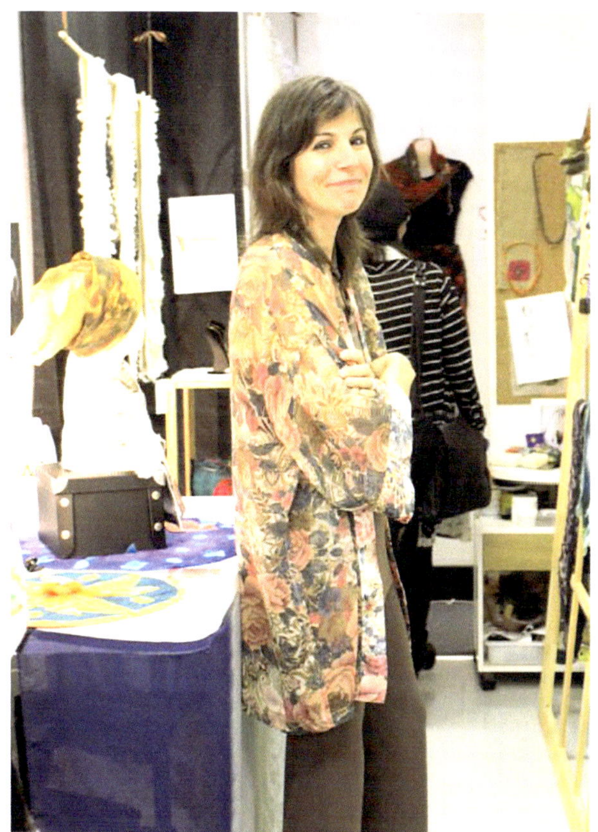

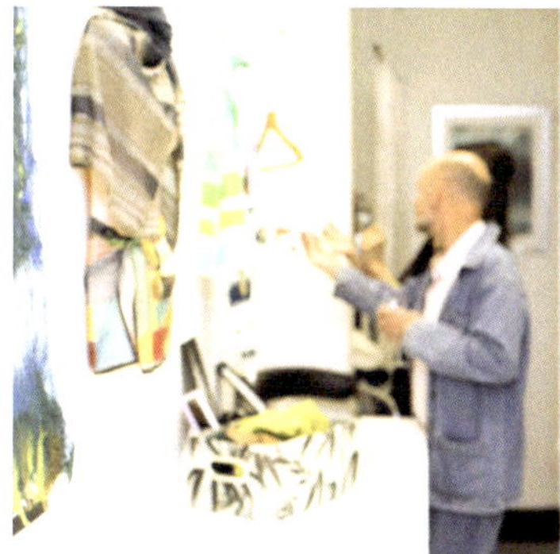

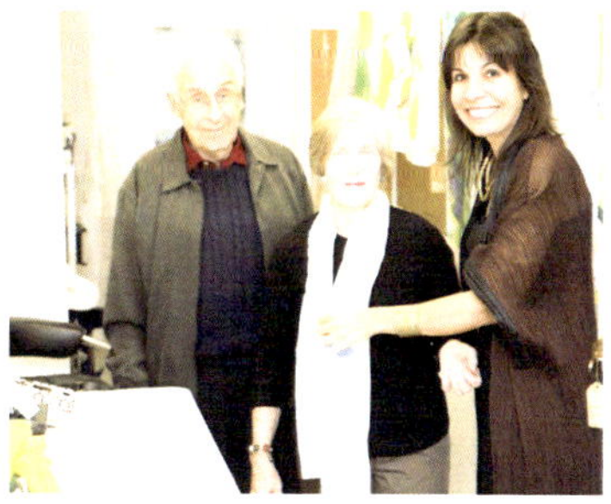

I love showing people around the studio on open days. People love to talk about art and felting.

www.ingramcontent.com/pod-product-compliance
Lightning Source LLC
LaVergne TN
LVRC090253110826
845147LV00007B/734

9780987541802